Amigurumi
ON THE GO

30 PATTERNS FOR CROCHETING KIDS' BAGS, BACKPACKS, AND MORE

Ana Paula Rímoli

Martingale®

Create with Confidence

Mission Statement

Dedicated to providing quality products and service to inspire creativity.

Credits

President & CEO: Tom Wierzbicki

Editor in Chief: Mary V. Green

Design Director: Paula Schlosser

Managing Editor: Karen Costello Soltys

Technical Editor: Ursula Reikes

Copy Editor: Melissa Bryan

Production Manager: Regina Girard

Illustrators: Christine Erikson, Ann Marra, & Adrienne Smitke

Cover & Text Designer: Adrienne Smitke

Photographer: Brent Kane

Special thanks to Land of Nod for generously allowing us to borrow their furniture and products as props.

Amigurumi On the Go:
30 Patterns for Crocheting Kids' Bags, Backpacks, and More
© 2012 by Ana Paula Rímoli

Create with Confidence

Martingale®
19021 120th Ave. NE, Ste. 102
Bothell, WA 98011-9511 USA
ShopMartingale.com

Printed in China
17 16 15 14 13 12   8 7 6 5 4 3 2 1

Library of Congress Cataloging-in-Publication Data
is available upon request.

ISBN: 978-1-60468-213-7

Dedication

- Para mis amigos queridos, que están lejos, pero siempre cerquita. Los quiero mucho.

- Para mis nenas lindas y el amor de mi vida.

Contents

Introduction

As many of you already know, I'm the mom of two little (and they'll always be little for me) girls: Martina, who is almost five and a half as this book goes to print, and Oli, who's just a few months from turning nine. Marti started kindergarten this year, and I really wasn't ready for my "baby" to be at school for so long every day. She, on the other hand, was more than ready, and loves her teachers, her new friends, and even homework! Oli has turned into a mini teenager who's all into reading nonstop, listening to music in her room, and painting her fingernails purple!

They are still arguing like crazy, and there's still a lot of yelling and paper cutting and crafting and reading, but it seems like time is going faster than ever. I guess I'm getting old! When I was little, a week seemed to last a year, and summer vacation was never ending. Now, I often feel like all I do is tell them, "Hurry up, you're going to be late for school," and "Stop fighting!" and "Clean up your room," and I'm so tired that days go by without really stopping to enjoy them. So what if they're late to school? (Don't tell them I said that.) So what if their room is full of books and clothes and dolls all over the place?

I cannot believe they are such little grown-ups, and I've decided to be a bit more mindful of them every day, because time seems to go way too fast. I don't even want to think about the day when they won't want to be with me all the time. In the meantime, though, I'll make them as many bags and little pouches and accessories as I can so that they'll always carry a reminder of me, and I can always be with them. Hey, what do you think about secretly putting a GPS device in the stuffing? Maybe a little camera? OK, maybe not!

I hope you have fun making the projects in the book for the kids in your life, or even for yourself! I really like the Colorful Little Duffel . . . in fact, I'm using mine! (If anything, I can always pretend it belongs to one of the girls.)

Thank you very much for giving these amigurumi-inspired projects a try, and for liking my work. Big hug, and happy crocheting!

-Ana

Backpacks

Finished Size

Approx 17" from top of head to beg of bag bottom

> My younger daughter, Martina, is already five and going to kindergarten—she's loving it, while I'm in denial. What happened to my little baby?! I made her the bear backpack to take to school, because even though she's such a "big girl," she still needs a teddy to keep her company.

Materials

Worsted-weight yarn in tan, brown, pink, and black, plus desired colors for head and extremities (approx 400 yds for bag/body and 200 yds for head and extremities)

Size J/10 (6 mm) crochet hook

Small pieces of tan, white, and black craft felt

Sewing thread and sharp needle

Black and pink embroidery floss and embroidery needle

Tapestry needle

7"-long zipper

Fiberfill or stuffing of your choice

Head

R1: Using tan, brown, pink, or black yarn, ch 2, 6 sc in second ch from hook.

R2: Sc 2 in each sc around. (12 sts)

R3: *Sc 1, 2 sc in next sc*, rep 6 times. (18 sts)

R4: *Sc 2, 2 sc in next sc*, rep 6 times. (24 sts)

R5: *Sc 3, 2 sc in next sc*, rep 6 times. (30 sts)

R6: *Sc 4, 2 sc in next sc*, rep 6 times. (36 sts)

R7: *Sc 5, 2 sc in next sc*, rep 6 times. (42 sts)

R8: *Sc 6, 2 sc in next sc*, rep 6 times. (48 sts)

R9: *Sc 7, 2 sc in next sc*, rep 6 times. (54 sts)

R10: *Sc 8, 2 sc in next sc*, rep 6 times. (60 sts)

R11: *Sc 9, 2 sc in next sc*, rep 6 times. (66 sts)

R12: *Sc 10, 2 sc in next sc*, rep 6 times. (72 sts)

R13: *Sc 11, 2 sc in next sc*, rep 6 times. (78 sts)

R14: *Sc 12, 2 sc in next sc*, rep 6 times. (84 sts)

R15–37: Sc 84.

R38: *Sc 12, dec 1*, rep 6 times. (78 sts)

R39: *Sc 11, dec 1*, rep 6 times. (72 sts)

R40: *Sc 10, dec 1*, rep 6 times.
(66 sts)

R41: *Sc 9, dec 1*, rep 6 times.
(60 sts)

Work on face. Use patterns on
page 15. For bear, monkey,
and bunny, cut muzzle from felt,
embroider nose and smile, and
sew in place. Cut eye pieces from
black felt, and sew in place.

For penguin, cut eye pieces from
black and white felt, sew black
pieces to white pieces, and sew

in place. Crochet and sew beak in
place (page 14).

R42: *Sc 8, dec 1*, rep 6 times.
(54 sts)

R43: *Sc 7, dec 1*, rep 6 times.
(48 sts)

R44: *Sc 6, dec 1*, rep 6 times.
(42 sts)

R45: *Sc 5, dec 1*, rep 6 times.
(36 sts)

R46: *Sc 4, dec 1*, rep 6 times.
(30 sts)

R47: *Sc 3, dec 1*, rep 6 times.
(24 sts)

R48: *Sc 2, dec 1*, rep 6 times.
(18 sts)

Stuff head.

R49: *Sc 1, dec 1*, rep 6 times.
(12 sts)

R50: *Sk 1 sc, sc 1*, rep 6 times.
(6 sts)

Fasten off and weave in end.

Bag/Body

Start crocheting the bag at the bottom.

R1: Using desired yarn color, ch 2, 6 sc in second ch from hook.

R2: Sc 2 in each sc around. (12 sts)

R3: *Sc 1, 2 sc in next sc*, rep 6 times. (18 sts)

R4: *Sc 2, 2 sc in next sc*, rep 6 times. (24 sts)

R5: *Sc 3, 2 sc in next sc*, rep 6 times. (30 sts)

R6: *Sc 4, 2 sc in next sc*, rep 6 times. (36 sts)

R7: *Sc 5, 2 sc in next sc*, rep 6 times. (42 sts)

R8: *Sc 6, 2 sc in next sc*, rep 6 times. (48 sts)

R9: *Sc 7, 2 sc in next sc*, rep 6 times. (54 sts)

R10: *Sc 8, 2 sc in next sc*, rep 6 times. (60 sts)

R11: *Sc 9, 2 sc in next sc*, rep 6 times. (66 sts)

R12: *Sc 10, 2 sc in next sc*, rep 6 times. (72 sts)

R13: *Sc 11, 2 sc in next sc*, rep 6 times. (78 sts)

R14: *Sc 12, 2 sc in next sc*, rep 6 times. (84 sts)

R15–16: Sc 84.

R17: Sc 84 through back loops only; this is last rnd of bottom.

Beg body as follows.

Using desired yarn color(s), create stripes as follows or as desired.

Bear: Alternate 5 rnds each of light blue, yellow, and off-white with 2 rnds of dark blue, finish with yellow.

Monkey: Alternate 8 rnds of red with 8 rnds of orange, finish with orange.

Bunny: Work (10 rnds of green, 1 rnd of white, 1 rnd of green, 1 rnd of white) 3 times, finish with green.

Penguin: Cont with bottom color.

R18–40: Sc 84.

We will now work on the front pocket.

R41: Sc 33, ch 18, sk 18 sts, sc 33.

R42: Sc 33, sc 18 in 18-ch space, sc 33. (84 sts)

Make pocket insert (page 12).

R43–52: Sc 84.

R53: *Sc 12, dec 1*, rep 6 times. (78 sts)

R54 and 55: Sc 78.

R56: *Sc 11, dec 1*, rep 6 times. (72 sts)

R57 and 58: Sc 72.

R59: *Sc 10, dec 1*, rep 6 times. (66 sts)

R60: Sc 66.

We will now leave a space to sew the zipper, so the instructions might seem a little weird because we will be leaving a space at the end of one rnd and the beg of the other one. Just trust me and follow these instructions!

R61 and 62: Sc 54, ch 24, sk 24 sts (half of skipped sts are at end of R61 and half in beg of R62), sc 42, sc 12 in first half of 24-ch space.

R63: Sc 12 in second half of 24-ch space, sc 54. (66 sts)

R64–70: Sc 66.

Sl st 1 and fasten off, leaving long tail for sewing.

Sew zipper in place (see page 76). Sew top of bag to R40 of head, which has 66 sts around.

POCKET INSERT

Using desired yarn color (I used a contrasting color), loosely ch 22.

Row 1: Sc 21 starting at second ch from hook, turn.

Rows 2–22: Ch 1, sc 21, turn.

Fasten off, leaving long tail for sewing. Turn bag inside out, and align the pocket piece with the opening you left in R42 of the bag. Sew all around the perimeter. Pocket made!

Sew pocket to wrong side of front.

Bear Ears (Make 2.)

R1: Using tan yarn, ch 2, 5 sc in second ch from hook.

R2: Sc 2 in each sc around. (10 sts)

R3–7: Sc 10.

Sl st 1 and fasten off, leaving long tail for sewing. Sew to sides of head beg at R14.

Monkey Ears (Make 2.)

R1: Using brown yarn, ch 2, 5 sc in second ch from hook.

R2: Sc 2 in each sc around. (10 sts)

R3: *Sc 1, 2 sc in next sc*, rep 5 times. (15 sts)

R4: *Sc 2, 2 sc in next sc*, rep 5 times. (20 sts)

R5–7: Sc 20.

Sl st 1 and fasten off, leaving long tail for sewing. Sew to sides of head beg at R22.

Bear and Monkey Arms and Legs (Make 2 of each.)

Use tan yarn for bear, or brown yarn for monkey. Switch to body colors at R16 if you want arms to have sleeves (like the bear).

R1: Ch 2, 6 sc in second ch from hook.

R2: Sc 2 in each sc around. (12 sts)

R3: *Sc 1, 2 sc in next sc*, rep 6 times. (18 sts)

R4–23: Sc 18.

Sl st 1 and fasten off, leaving long tail for sewing. Stuff a little and sew open end closed. Sew arms 2 rnds below body/head join at each side. Sew legs to bottom, approx 4" apart, as shown on facing page.

Bunny Ears (Make 2.)

R1: Using pink yarn, ch 2, 5 sc in second ch from hook.

R2: Sc 2 in each sc around. (10 sts)

R3: *Sc 1, 2 sc in next sc*, rep 5 times. (15 sts)

R4: *Sc 2, 2 sc in next sc*, rep 5 times. (20 sts)

R5–23: Sc 20.

Sl st 1 and fasten off, leaving long tail for sewing. Sew to sides of head beg at R8.

Bunny Arms and Legs (Make 2 of each.)

R1: Using pink yarn, ch 2, 5 sc in second ch from hook.

R2: Sc 2 in each sc around. (10 sts)

R3: *Sc 1, 2 sc in next sc*, rep 5 times. (15 sts)

ARMS

R4–16: Sc 15.

LEGS

R4–10: Sc 15.

FOR BOTH

Sl st 1 and fasten off, leaving long tail for sewing. Stuff a little and sew open end tog. Sew arms 2 rows below body/head join at each side. Sew legs to bottom at R17 approx 5" apart.

Penguin Wings (Make 2.)

R1: Using black yarn, ch 2, 6 sc in second ch from hook.

R2: Sc 2 in each sc around. (12 sts)

R3: Sc 12.

R4: *Sc 1, 2 sc in next sc*, rep 6 times. (18 sts)

R5: Sc 18.

R6: *Sc 2, 2 sc in next sc*, rep 6 times. (24 sts)

R7–19: Sc 24.

R20: *Sc 2, dec 1*, rep 6 times. (18 sts)

R21 and 22: Sc 18.

Sl st 1 and fasten off, leaving long tail for sewing. Sew open end tog and sew wings 2 rnds below body/head join at each side.

Penguin Feet (Make 2.)

R1: Using orange yarn, ch 2, 5 sc in second ch from hook.

R2: Sc 2 in each sc around. (10 sts)

R3: *Sc 1, 2 sc in next sc*, rep 5 times. (15 sts)

R4–8: Sc 15.

Sl st 1 and fasten off, leaving long tail for sewing. Sew to body at R17, approx 4½" apart.

Penguin Earmuffs

Earmuffs consist of 2 ear pads and a separate headband.

EAR PADS (MAKE 2.)

R1: Using yellow yarn, ch 2, 6 sc in second ch from hook.

R2: Sc 2 in each sc around. (12 sts)

R3: *Sc 1, 2 sc in next sc*, rep 6 times. (18 sts)

R4: *Sc 2, 2 sc in next sc*, rep 6 times. (24 sts)

R5–7: Sc 24.

Sl st 1 and fasten off, leaving long tail for sewing. Stuff and sew to sides of head beg at R21.

HEADBAND

Using yellow yarn, loosely ch 35.

Row 1: Sc 34 starting in second ch from hook, turn.

Row 2: Ch 1, sc 34.

Fasten off and sew between ear pads.

Penguin Beak

R1: Using orange yarn, ch 2, 5 sc in second ch from hook.

R2: Sc 2 in each sc around. (10 sts)

R3: *Sc 1, 2 sc in next sc*, rep 5 times. (15 sts)

R4 and 5: Sc 15.

Sl st 1 and fasten off, leaving long tail for sewing. Sew to head.

Straps (Make 2.)

Using desired yarn color and leaving a long tail for sewing, loosely ch 76.

Row 1: Sc 75 starting at second ch from hook, turn.

Rows 2–4: Ch 1, sc 75, turn.

Row 5: Sl st 75.

Fasten off, leaving long tail for sewing. Sew one end of each strap to back of head at R17, approx 3" apart. Sew other end to back of bottom at R17, approx 4" to 5" apart.

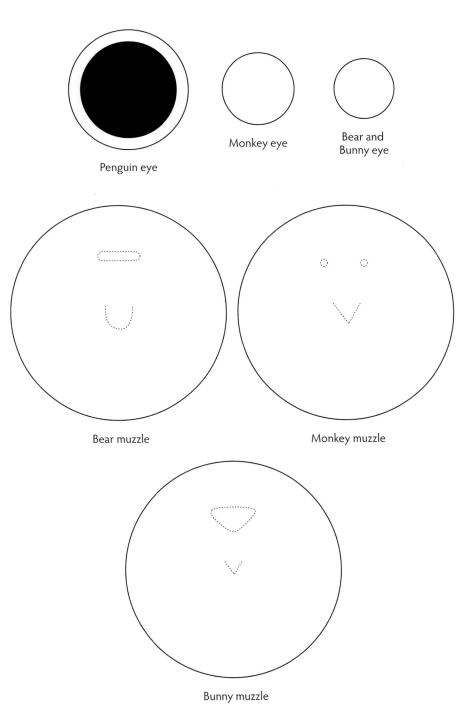

Penguin eye

Monkey eye

Bear and
Bunny eye

Bear muzzle

Monkey muzzle

Bunny muzzle

Pencil Cases

Finished Size

Approx 4½" high x 7¼" wide

> I've always liked school supplies. I get happy just smelling the new notebooks and pencils, and Oli (my eight-year-old) is the same way. I figured it'd be nice for her to have a cute pencil case for storing her things and taking them to school.

Materials

Worsted-weight yarn in pink, tan, brown, and black, plus a bit of orange (approx 110 yds per pencil case)

Size J/10 (6 mm) crochet hook

Small pieces of tan, white, and black craft felt

Sewing thread and sharp needle

Black and pink embroidery floss and embroidery needle

Tapestry needle

7"-long zipper

Tiny bit of fiberfill or stuffing of your choice

Case

The case is worked in the round from the bottom.

Using pink, tan, brown, or black yarn, loosely ch 31.

R1: Sc 30 starting at second bump at back of ch (see page 74), then work 30 sc on opposite side of ch (front loops of ch). (60 sts)

R2–24: Sc 60.

Sl st 1 and fasten off.

Face

Use patterns on page 19.

For bunny, bear, and monkey, cut muzzle from felt, embroider nose and smile; sew approx ¾ of the way around, stuff a little, and finish sewing. Cut eye pieces from black felt and sew in place.

For penguin, cut eye pieces from black and white felt, sew black pieces to white pieces slightly off center, and sew in place.

Bunny and Bear Ears (Make 2.)

R1: Using pink for the bunny or tan for the bear, ch 2, sc 6 in second ch from hook.

R2: Sc 2 in every sc around. (12 sts)

For bunny:
R3–10: Sc 12.

For bear:

R3–6: Sc 12.

Sl st 1 and fasten off, leaving long tail for sewing. Sew open end tog and sew to last rnd on the back.

Monkey Ears (Make 2.)

R1: Using brown yarn, ch 2, sc 6 in second ch from hook.

R2: Sc 2 in every sc around. (12 sts)

R3: *Sc 1, 2 sc in next sc*, rep 6 times. (18 sts)

R4–7: Sc 18.

Sl st 1 and fasten off, leaving long tail for sewing. Sew open end tog and sew to each side.

Penguin Beak

R1: Using orange yarn, ch 2, sc 6 in second ch from hook.

R2: Sc 2 in every sc around. (12 sts)

R3: *Sc 1, 2 sc in next sc*, rep 6 times. (18 sts)

R4–6: Sc 18.

Sl st 1 and fasten off, leaving long tail for sewing. Stuff a little and sew between eyes.

Zipper

Sew zipper in place (see page 76).

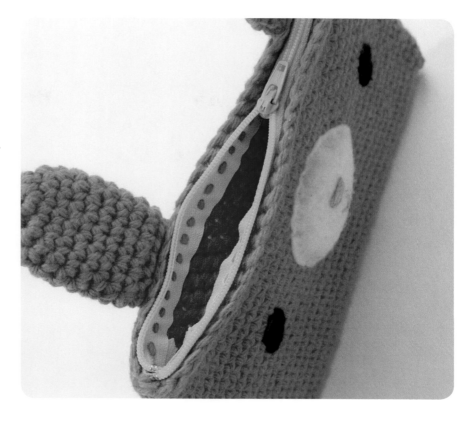

Penguin eye

Bear, Bunny, and Monkey eye

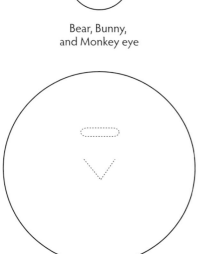

Bear muzzle

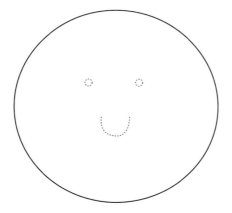

Monkey muzzle

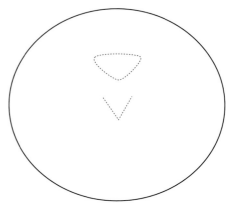

Bunny muzzle

Roundie Bags

Finished Size

Approx 6" diameter

These are the perfect size for Martina to take her little toys everywhere. I bet that an older kid (or grown-up!) could also use one to carry the necessities for a quick outing: there's more than enough space for a little money, lip balm, and even a small snack.

Materials

Worsted-weight yarn in white, gray, yellow, red, black, green, and brown (approx 110 yds per bag)

Size J/10 (6 mm) crochet hook

Small pieces of white and black craft felt

Sewing thread and sharp needle

Black embroidery floss and embroidery needle

Tapestry needle

9"-long zipper

Bag Back and Front (Make 2.)

R1: Using white, gray, yellow, or red yarn, ch 2, sc 5 in second ch from hook.

R2: Sc 2 in every sc around. (10 sts)

R3: *Sc 1, sc 2 in next sc*, rep 5 times. (15 sts)

R4: *Sc 2, sc 2 in next sc*, rep 5 times. (20 sts)

R5: *Sc 3, sc 2 in next sc*, rep 5 times. (25 sts)

R6: *Sc 4, sc 2 in next sc*, rep 5 times. (30 sts)

R7: *Sc 5, sc 2 in next sc*, rep 5 times. (35 sts)

R8: *Sc 6, sc 2 in next sc*, rep 5 times. (40 sts)

R9: *Sc 7, sc 2 in next sc*, rep 5 times. (45 sts)

R10: *Sc 8, sc 2 in next sc*, rep 5 times. (50 sts)

R11: *Sc 9, sc 2 in next sc*, rep 5 times. (55 sts)

R12: *Sc 10, sc 2 in next sc*, rep 5 times. (60 sts)

R13: *Sc 11, sc 2 in next sc*, rep 5 times. (65 sts)

R14: *Sc 12, sc 2 in next sc*, rep 5 times. (70 sts)

R15 and 16: Sc 70.

Sl st 1 and fasten off; weave in ends.

WORK ON FACE

Use patterns on page 24.

For panda, cut muzzle from white felt, embroider nose and smile, and sew in place. Cut eye pieces from white and black felt, sew small black pieces to white pieces, sew to smaller end of large black pieces, and sew in place.

For koala, cut nose from black felt and sew in place. Embroider smile below nose. Cut eye pieces from black felt and sew in place.

For cat, cut muzzle from white felt, embroider nose and smile, and sew in place. Cut eye pieces from black felt and sew in place. Cut triangle pieces from white felt and sew in place around face.

For apple, cut eye pieces from black felt and sew in place. Embroider smile.

JOIN FRONT AND BACK

Sew zipper between front and back (see page 76). With WS tog, and yarn to match purse, sew remainder of front and back tog.

Panda Ears (Make 2.)

R1: Using black yarn, ch 2, sc 6 in second ch from hook.

R2: Sc 2 in every sc around. (12 sts)

R3–6: Sc 12.

Sl st 1 and fasten off, leaving long tail for sewing. Sew open end tog and sew to last rnd on back, approx 4" apart.

Koala Ears (Make 2.)

R1: Using gray yarn, ch 2, sc 5 in second ch from hook.

R2: Sc 2 in every sc around. (10 sts)

R3: *Sc 1, sc 2 in next sc*, rep 5 times. (15 sts)

R4: *Sc 2, sc 2 in next sc*, rep 5 times. (20 sts)

R5–10: Sc 20.

Sl st 1 and fasten off, leaving long tail for sewing. Sew open end tog and sew to last rnd on back, approx 4" apart.

Cat Ears (Make 2.)

R1: Using yellow yarn, ch 2, sc 6 in second ch from hook.

R2: Sc 6.

R3: Sc 2 in every sc around. (12 sts)

R4: Sc 12.

R5: *Sc 1, 2 sc in next sc*, rep 6 times. (18 sts)

R6–8: Sc 18.

Sl st 1 and fasten off, leaving long tail for sewing. Sew open end tog and sew to last rnd on back, approx 4" apart.

Apple Leaf

R1: Using green yarn, ch 2, sc 5 in second ch from hook.

R2: Sc 2 in every sc around. (10 sts)

R3–7: Sc 10.

R8: Dec 5 times. (5 sts)

Fasten off, leaving long tail to close up 5-st hole. Sew to zipper pull.

Handle

Using red yarn for the panda, green for the koala, white for the cat, or brown for the apple, loosely ch 21.

Row 1: Sc 20 starting in second ch from hook, turn.

Rows 2 and 3: Ch 1, sc 20, turn.

Fasten off, leaving long tail for sewing. Sew ends to back, approx 1" below zipper and 3" apart.

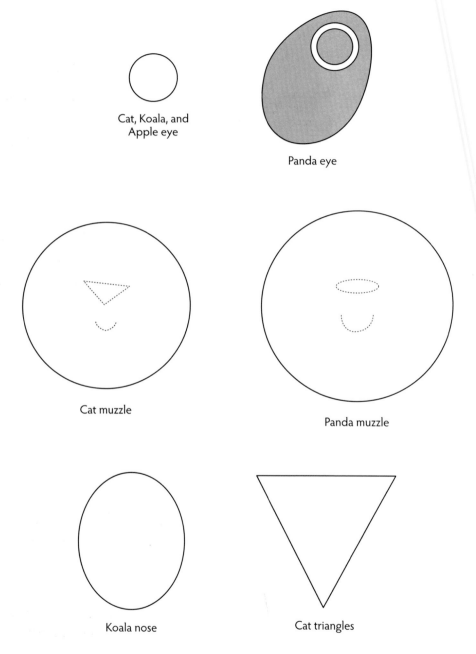

Cat, Koala, and
Apple eye

Panda eye

Cat muzzle

Panda muzzle

Koala nose

Cat triangles

Octopus Bag

Finished Size

Approx 6" high, without legs; 10" high with legs

> Some years ago I made a little octopus bag, and I've been meaning to make a bigger one for the longest time. This is it, at last! It's the perfect size to take for a playdate—let your youngster fill it up with toys, an extra sweater, or some cookies to share.

Materials

Worsted-weight yarn in light pink (approx 75 yds) and dark pink (approx 250 yds)

Size J/10 (6 mm) crochet hook

Small piece of black craft felt

Sewing thread and sharp needle

Black embroidery floss and embroidery needle

Tapestry needle

7"-long zipper

Cheeks (Make 2.)

R1: Using light-pink yarn, ch 2, 5 sc in second ch from hook.

R2: Sc 2 in each sc around. (10 sts)

R3: *Sc 1, 2 sc in next sc*, rep 5 times. (15 sts)

Sl st 1 and fasten off, leaving long tail for sewing. Set aside.

Bag/Body

Start crocheting the bag at the bottom.

R1: Using dark-pink yarn, ch 2, 6 sc in second ch from hook.

R2: Sc 2 in each sc around. (12 sts)

R3: *Sc 1, 2 sc in next sc*, rep 6 times. (18 sts)

R4: *Sc 2, 2 sc in next sc*, rep 6 times. (24 sts)

R5: *Sc 3, 2 sc in next sc*, rep 6 times. (30 sts)

R6: *Sc 4, 2 sc in next sc*, rep 6 times. (36 sts)

R7: *Sc 5, 2 sc in next sc*, rep 6 times. (42 sts)

R8: *Sc 6, 2 sc in next sc*, rep 6 times. (48 sts)

R9: *Sc 7, 2 sc in next sc*, rep 6 times. (54 sts)

R10: *Sc 8, 2 sc in next sc*, rep 6 times. (60 sts)

R11: *Sc 9, 2 sc in next sc*, rep 6 times. (66 sts)

R12: *Sc 10, 2 sc in next sc*, rep 6 times. (72 sts)

R13–39: Sc 72.

R40: *Sc 10, dec 1*, rep 6 times. (66 sts)

We will now work on the opening for the zipper.

R41: Ch 24, sk 24 sts, sc 42.

R42: Sc 24 in ch-24 space, sc 42.

Cont with body.

R43: *Sc 9, dec 1*, rep 6 times. (60 sts)

R44: *Sc 8, dec 1*, rep 6 times. (54 sts)

R45: *Sc 7, dec 1*, rep 6 times. (48 sts)

R46: *Sc 6, dec 1*, rep 6 times. (42 sts)

Sew zipper in place (see page 76).

Work on face. Use pattern at right. Cut eye pieces from black felt. Holding bag with top edge facing up, sew in place, and embroider smile. Sew cheeks in place.

R47: *Sc 5, dec 1*, rep 6 times. (36 sts)

R48: *Sc 4, dec 1*, rep 6 times. (30 sts)

R49: *Sc 3, dec 1*, rep 6 times. (24 sts)

R50: *Sc 2, dec 1*, rep 6 times. (18 sts)

R51: *Sc 1, dec 1*, rep 6 times. (12 sts)

R52: Dec 6 times. (6 sts)

Fasten off, leaving long tail to close up 6-st hole.

Arms (Make 8.)

Starting with dark-pink yarn, alternate 2 rnds of dark pink and 2 rnds of light pink.

R1: Ch 2, sc 5 in second ch from hook.

R2: Sc 2 in every sc around. (10 sts)

R3: *Sc 1, sc 2 in next sc*, rep 5 times. (15 sts)

R4–18: Sc 15.

Sl st 1 and fasten off, leaving long tail for sewing. Sew open end tog and sew arms evenly spaced around bottom of bag at R13.

Strap

Using light-pink yarn, loosely ch 152.

Row 1: Hdc 150 starting in third ch from hook, turn.

Row 2: Ch 2, hdc 150, turn.

Row 3: Ch 1, sc 150.

Fasten off, leaving long tail for sewing. Sew ends of strap to opposite sides of bag at R37.

Octopus eye

Owl Book Bag

Finished Size

Approx 10" wide x 11¾" tall

> *I love this bag, and I have one of my own! Oli wants one too (I have to start working on it), to take to school on the days she doesn't have to carry those big, heavy books (schoolkids these days and their poor little backs!). It'd be perfect to take on the bus or to the beach, with enough space for a couple magazines, some books, and lots of pencils to do word puzzles!*

Materials

Worsted-weight yarn in dark blue and light blue (approx 210 yds *each*) and small amounts of white and orange

Size J/10 (6 mm) crochet hook

Small pieces of orange and black craft felt

Sewing thread and sharp needle

Tapestry needle

Bag

The bag is crocheted in the round starting at the bottom.

Using dark-blue yarn, loosely ch 39.

R1: Sc 38 starting at second bump at back of ch (see page 74), then work 38 sc on opposite side of ch (front loops of ch). (76 sts)

R2: *Sc 3 in next sc, sc 37*, rep once. (80 sts)

R3: *(Sc 2 in next sc) 3 times, sc 37*, rep once. (86 sts)

R4–6: Sc 86.

R7: Sc 65, change to light-blue yarn, sc 21.

R8–43: Starting with light blue, alternate 2 rnds of light blue and two rnds of dark blue.

Change to light-blue yarn.

R44–61: Sc 86.

Sl st 1 and fasten off.

Eye Roundies
(Make 2 of each color.)

Each eye is made of two crocheted circles, with a felt circle sewn in the middle.

OUTER PIECE OF THE EYE

R1: Using white yarn, ch 2, sc 5 in second ch from hook.

R2: Sc 2 in every sc around. (10 sts)

R3: *Sc 1, 2 sc in next sc*, rep 5 times. (15 sts)

R4: *Sc 2, 2 sc in next sc*, rep 5 times. (20 sts)

R5: *Sc 3, 2 sc in next sc*, rep 5 times. (25 sts)

R6: *Sc 4, 2 sc in next sc*, rep 5 times. (30 sts)

R7: *Sc 5, 2 sc in next sc*, rep 5 times. (35 sts)

R8: *Sc 6, 2 sc in next sc*, rep 5 times. (40 sts)

R9: Sc 40.

Sl st 1 and fasten off, leaving long tail for sewing. Set aside.

MIDDLE PIECE OF THE EYE

R1: Using dark-blue yarn, ch 2, sc 5 in second ch from hook.

R2: Sc 2 in every sc around. (10 sts)

R3: *Sc 1, 2 sc in next sc*, rep 5 times. (15 sts)

R4: *Sc 2, 2 sc in next sc*, rep 5 times. (20 sts)

R5: *Sc 3, 2 sc in next sc*, rep 5 times. (25 sts)

R6: *Sc 4, 2 sc in next sc*, rep 5 times. (30 sts)

Sl st 1 and fasten off, leaving long tail for sewing.

INNER PIECE OF THE EYE

Using the pattern on facing page, cut eye pieces from black felt and sew each one to the center of a blue roundie.

Sew each blue roundie slightly off center to a white roundie, and sew the complete eye units in place on bag.

Beak

Using the pattern, cut two diamonds from orange felt, layer one on top of the other, and sew together all around the edges. Fold beak in half to create a crease, and sew to bag along the crease (so the owl can talk!).

Sew 2 pieces together.

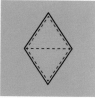
Sew onto bag.

Wings/Side Pockets (Make 2.)

R1: Using dark-blue yarn, ch 2, sc 6 in second ch from hook.

R2: Sc 2 in every sc around. (12 sts)

R3: *Sc 1, 2 sc in next sc*, rep 6 times. (18 sts)

R4: *Sc 2, 2 sc in next sc*, rep 6 times. (24 sts)

R5: *Sc 3, 2 sc in next sc*, rep 6 times. (30 sts)

R6: *Sc 4, 2 sc in next sc*, rep 6 times. (36 sts)

R7: *Sc 5, 2 sc in next sc*, rep 6 times. (42 sts)

R8: *Sc 6, 2 sc in next sc*, rep 6 times. (48 sts)

R9: *Sc 7, 2 sc in next sc*, rep 6 times. (54 sts)

R10: *Sc 8, 2 sc in next sc*, rep 6 times. (60 sts)

R11: *Sc 9, 2 sc in next sc*, rep 6 times. (66 sts)

R12: Sc 66.

R13: *3 sc in next sc, sk 1 sc, sl st 1*, rep until end.

Fasten off, leaving long tail for sewing. Place pockets on sides of bag at the bottom, so half is on front and half is on back. Stitching in R12 of pocket, sew approx ¾ of the way around, leaving opening at the top on both front and back.

Leave open.

Inside Pocket

Using dark-blue yarn, loosely ch 31.

Row 1: Sc 30 starting in second ch from hook, turn.

Rows 2–25: Ch 1, sc 30, turn.

Fasten off, and sew to inside of bag on 3 sides, leaving top open.

Handles (Make 2.)

Using orange yarn and leaving a long tail for sewing later, loosely ch 71.

Row 1: Sc 70 starting in second ch from hook, turn.

Rows 2 and 3: Ch 1, sc 70, turn.

Fasten off, leaving long tail for sewing.

Measure the width of your handle. Cut two long strips from orange felt to line the handles. (If you're using a rectangle of craft felt, you'll need more than one strip.) Sew the lining neatly to the back of each handle. Sew ends of a handle 2½" from each side on front and back of bag.

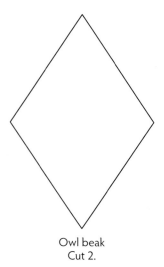

Owl beak
Cut 2.

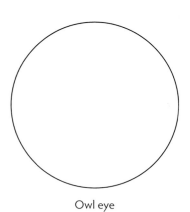

Owl eye

Little Mushroom Purse

Finished Size

Approx 6" high

This precious purse is small enough to carry little toys, cute enough to take everywhere!

Materials

Worsted-weight yarn in red and white (approx 90 total yds)

Size J/10 (6 mm) crochet hook

Small pieces of white and black craft felt

Sewing thread and sharp needle

Black embroidery floss and embroidery needle

Tapestry needle

7"-long zipper

Purse

Start crocheting the purse at the top.

R1: Using red yarn, ch 2, 7 sc in second ch from hook.

R2: Sc 2 in each sc around. (14 sts)

R3: *Sc 1, 2 sc in next sc*, rep 7 times. (21 sts)

R4: *Sc 2, 2 sc in next sc*, rep 7 times. (28 sts)

R5: *Sc 3, 2 sc in next sc*, rep 7 times. (35 sts)

R6: *Sc 4, 2 sc in next sc*, rep 7 times. (42 sts)

R7: *Sc 5, 2 sc in next sc*, rep 7 times. (49 sts)

R8: *Sc 6, 2 sc in next sc*, rep 7 times. (56 sts)

R9–12: Sc 56.

We will now work on the opening for the zipper.

R13: Ch 26, sk 26 sts, sc 30.

R14: Sc 26 in the 26-ch space, sc 30. (56 sts)

Cont with purse.

R15–21: Sc 56.

Sew zipper in place (see page 76).

R22: *Sc 6, dec 1*, rep 7 times. (49 sts)

R23: *Sc 5, dec 1*, rep 7 times. (42 sts)

R24: *Sc 4, dec 1*, rep 7 times. (35 sts)

R25: *Sc 3, dec 1*, rep 7 times. (28 sts)

R26: *Sc 2, dec 1*, rep 7 times. (21 sts)

Handle

Using white yarn, loosely ch 34.

Dc 32 starting in third ch from hook.

Fasten off, leaving long tail for sewing. Sew ends tog, and sew on same rnd as zipper.

Using the pattern at right, cut 5 spots from white felt and sew them on the mushroom. If desired, you can cut one in half and sew a half on either side of the zipper.

Change to white yarn.

R27–31: Sc 21.

R32: *Sc 2, 2 sc in next sc*, rep 7 times. (28 sts)

R33: Sc 28.

Work on face. Use pattern at right. Cut eye pieces from black felt, sew to face, and embroider smile.

R34: Sc 28 through back loops only.

R35: *Sc 2, dec 1*, rep 7 times. (21 sts)

R36: *Sc 1, dec 1*, rep 7 times. (14 sts)

R37: *Sk 1 sc, sc 1*, rep 7 times. (7 sts)

Fasten off, leaving long tail to close up 7-st hole.

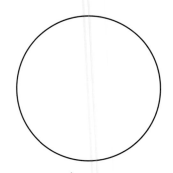

Mushroom spot

Mushroom eye

Whale Bag

Finished Size

Approx 17" long from nose to end of tail

> *I made this one thinking of Oli's sleepovers and visits to Grandma's house. It's big! Pajamas and extra clothes will fit comfortably, plus the little piggy she's been sleeping with since she was two. Don't forget the toothbrush!*

Materials

Worsted-weight yarn in light blue, plus small amounts of dark blue, yellow, and white (approx 400 total yds)

Size J/10 (6 mm) crochet hook

Small pieces of white and black craft felt

Sewing thread and sharp needle

Tapestry needle

12"-long zipper

Tiny bit of fiberfill or stuffing of your choice

Eye Roundies (Make 2.)

R1: Using dark-blue yarn, ch 2, sc 5 in second ch from hook.

R2: Sc 2 in every sc around. (10 sts)

R3: *Sc 1, 2 sc in next sc*, rep 5 times. (15 sts)

R4: *Sc 2, 2 sc in next sc*, rep 5 times. (20 sts)

R5: *Sc 3, 2 sc in next sc*, rep 5 times. (25 sts)

R6: Sc 25.

Sl st 1 and fasten off, leaving long tail for sewing.

Using the patterns on page 38, cut eye pieces from white and black felt. Referring to the photo on page 36, sew small white piece close to the edge of black piece. Then sew felt pieces to center of blue eye roundie, and set aside.

Body

R1: Using light-blue yarn, ch 2, sc 5 in second ch from hook.

R2: Sc 2 in every sc around. (10 sts)

R3: *Sc 1, 2 sc in next sc*, rep 5 times. (15 sts)

R4: *Sc 2, 2 sc in next sc*, rep 5 times. (20 sts)

R5: *Sc 3, 2 sc in next sc*, rep 5 times. (25 sts)

R6: *Sc 4, 2 sc in next sc*, rep 5 times. (30 sts)

R7: *Sc 5, 2 sc in next sc*, rep 5 times. (35 sts)

R8: *Sc 6, 2 sc in next sc*, rep 5 times. (40 sts)

R9: *Sc 7, 2 sc in next sc*, rep 5 times. (45 sts)

R10: *Sc 8, 2 sc in next sc*, rep 5 times. (50 sts)

R11: *Sc 9, 2 sc in next sc*, rep 5 times. (55 sts)

R12: *Sc 10, 2 sc in next sc*, rep 5 times. (60 sts)

R13: *Sc 11, 2 sc in next sc*, rep 5 times. (65 sts)

R14: *Sc 12, 2 sc in next sc*, rep 5 times. (70 sts)

R15: *Sc 13, 2 sc in next sc*, rep 5 times. (75 sts)

R16: *Sc 14, 2 sc in next sc*, rep 5 times. (80 sts)

R17: *Sc 15, 2 sc in next sc*, rep 5 times. (85 sts)

R18: *Sc 16, 2 sc in next sc*, rep 5 times. (90 sts)

R19: *Sc 17, 2 sc in next sc*, rep 5 times. (95 sts)

R20–24: Sc 95.

We will now work on the opening for the zipper:

R25: Ch 40, sk 40, sc 55.

R26: Sc 40 in 40-ch space, sc 55. (95 sts)

Cont with body.

R27–32: Sc 95.

Sew zipper in place (see page 76); the zipper will be the whale's mouth.

R33–38: Sc 95.

Work on face. Sew eyes in place, stuffing them a little bit.

R39–46: Sc 95.

R47: *Sc 17, dec 1*, rep 5 times. (90 sts)

R48: *Sc 16, dec 1*, rep 5 times. (85 sts)

R49–51: Sc 85.

R52: *Sc 15, dec 1*, rep 5 times. (80 sts)

R53: *Sc 14, dec 1*, rep 5 times. (75 sts)

R54 and 55: Sc 75.

R56: *Sc 13, dec 1*, rep 5 times. (70 sts)

R57: *Sc 12, dec 1*, rep 5 times. (65 sts)

R58–61: Sc 65.

R62: *Sc 11, dec 1*, rep 5 times. (60 sts)

R63: *Sc 10, dec 1*, rep 5 times. (55 sts)

R64–66: Sc 55.

R67: *Sc 9, dec 1*, rep 5 times. (50 sts)

R68: *Sc 8, dec 1*, rep 5 times. (45 sts)

R69–71: Sc 45.

R72: *Sc 7, dec 1*, rep 5 times. (40 sts)

R73: *Sc 6, dec 1*, rep 5 times. (35 sts)

R74: *Sc 5, dec 1*, rep 5 times. (30 sts)

R75: *Sc 4, dec 1*, rep 5 times. (25 sts)

R76: Sc 25.

R77: *Sc 3, dec 1*, rep 5 times. (20 sts)

R78: Sc 20.

R79: *Sc 2, dec 1*, rep 5 times. (15 sts)

R80: *Sc 1, dec 1*, rep 5 times. (10 sts)

R81: Dec 5 times. (5 sts)

Fasten off, leaving long tail to close up 5-st hole.

Flippers (Make 2.)

R1: Using light-blue yarn, ch 2, sc 5 in second ch from hook.

R2: Sc 2 in every sc around. (10 sts)

R3: Sc 10.

R4: *Sc 1, 2 sc in next sc*, rep 5 times. (15 sts)

R5: Sc 15.

R6: *Sc 2, 2 sc in next sc*, rep 5 times. (20 sts)

R7: Sc 20.

R8: *Sc 3, 2 sc in next sc*, rep 5 times. (25 sts)

R9–13: Sc 25.

Sl st 1 and fasten off, leaving long tail for sewing. Sew open end tog and sew to side of whale beg at R36.

Tail (Make 2.)

R1: Using light-blue yarn, ch 2, sc 5 in second ch from hook.

R2: Sc 2 in every sc around. (10 sts)

R3: Sc 10.

R4: *Sc 1, 2 sc in next sc*, rep 5 times. (15 sts)

R5: Sc 15.

R6: *Sc 2, 2 sc in next sc*, rep 5 times. (20 sts)

R7–12: Sc 20.

R13: *Sc 2, dec 1*, rep 5 times. (15 sts)

R14: *Sc 1, dec 1*, rep 5 times. (10 sts)

R15: Sc 10.

Sl st 1 and fasten off, leaving long tail for sewing. Sew open end tog. Sew 2 tails tog on last 3 rnds and sew joined tail to end of body.

Handle

Using yellow yarn, loosely ch 61.

Row 1: Sc 60 starting in second ch from hook, turn.

Rows 2–5: Sc 60, turn.

Fasten off (or see option on facing page), leaving long tail for sewing. Sew handle to top of whale body, one end at R22 and the other end at R48.

Water Spout

Using white yarn, *ch 18, sl st in first ch*, rep 3 times. (3 loops)

Fasten off and sew to top of whale body at R20.

Stripes on Whale's Belly

Using tapestry needle and yellow yarn, embroider lines from side to side with a backstitch, starting 2 rnds below the zipper. Stitch lines in every other rnd of sc, decreasing the line length as you get closer to the tail. My whale has 27 yellow belly stripes.

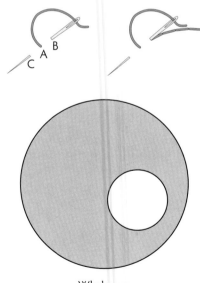

Whale eye

Optional Stronger Handle

I made the handle a little more durable by weaving the yarn back and forth between the rows of sc. To do this, do not fasten off. Cut the tail 4 times longer than the handle plus 8". Pull the end of the long tail through the last st. Then thread the tail onto a tapestry needle and working from left to right, weave the tail below the last row of sc you just did, going under one st and over the next. At the end of the row, turn, working from right to left, weave below the next row of sc, but alternate the over and under from the first row. Cont weaving below the next 2 rows; you'll have 4 total. Fasten off, leaving a long tail for sewing.

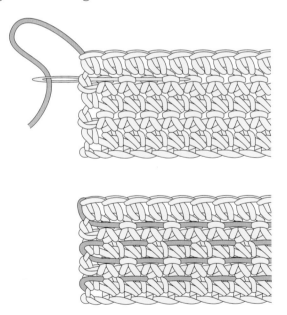

Little Owl Purse

Finished Size

Approx 7" high

I love owls, and really, what could be cuter than carrying a little owl with you wherever you go?

Materials

Worsted-weight yarn in tan, brown, orange, and yellow (approx 190 total yds)

Size J/10 (6 mm) crochet hook

Small piece of black craft felt

Sewing thread and sharp needle

Tapestry needle

7"-long zipper

Eye Roundies (Make 2.)

R1: Using yellow yarn, ch 3, 6 hdc in third chain from hook.

R2: 2 hdc in each hdc around. (12 sts)

R3: *Hdc 1, 2 hdc in next hdc*, rep 6 times. (18 sts)

R4: *Hdc 2, 2 hdc in next hdc*, rep 6 times. (24 sts)

Sl st 1 and fasten off, leaving long tail for sewing. Using the pattern on page 42, cut eye pieces from black felt and sew to middle of roundies; set aside.

Purse

Start crocheting at the top of the purse.

R1: Using brown yarn, ch 2, 7 sc in second ch from hook.

R2: Sc 2 in each sc around. (14 sts)

R3: *Sc 1, 2 sc in next sc*, rep 7 times. (21 sts)

R4: *Sc 2, 2 sc in next sc*, rep 7 times. (28 sts)

R5: *Sc 3, 2 sc in next sc*, rep 7 times. (35 sts)

R6: *Sc 4, 2 sc in next sc*, rep 7 times. (42 sts)

R7: *Sc 5, 2 sc in next sc*, rep 7 times. (49 sts)

R8–11: Sc 49.

We will now work on the opening for the zipper:

R12: Ch 22, sk 22 sts, sc 27.

R13: Sc 22 in the 22-ch space, sc 27. (49 sts)

Cont with purse.

R14 and 15: Sc 49.

Change to tan.

R16–23: Sc 49.

Work on face. Place eye roundies next to each other so that half is in the brown area and half is in the tan area; sew in place. Embroider beak between eyes with orange yarn.

Sew zipper in place (see page 76).

R24: *Sc 6, 2 sc in next sc*, rep 7 times. (56 sts)

R25–36: Sc 56.

R37: *Sc 6, dec 1*, rep 7 times. (49 sts)

R38: *Sc 5, dec 1*, rep 7 times. (42 sts)

R39: *Sc 4, dec 1*, rep 7 times. (35 sts)

R40: *Sc 3, dec 1*, rep 7 times. (28 sts)

R41: *Sc 2, dec 1*, rep 7 times. (21 sts)

R42: *Sc 1, dec 1*, rep 7 times. (14 sts)

R43: *Sk 1 sc, sc 1*, rep 7 times. (7 sts)

Fasten off, leaving long tail to close up 7-st hole.

Wings (Make 2.)

R1: Using brown yarn, ch 2, 8 sc in second ch from hook.

R2: Sc 2 in each sc around. (16 sts)

R3–14: Sc 16.

Fasten off, leaving long tail for sewing. Sew open end tog and sew to sides on last rnd of brown.

Handle

Using orange yarn and leaving a long tail for sewing later, loosely ch 81, turn.

Sc 80 starting in second ch from hook.

Fasten off, leaving long tail for sewing. Sew ends to sides of purse, 2 rnds above wings.

Owl eye

Fish Bag

Finished Size

Approx 12" long from nose to end of tail

Martina LOVES fish, and while I was working on the whale bag, she pretty much demanded I made a fish one. I couldn't let her down! Feel free to try different colors—and don't worry about whether those combinations really exist under the sea!

Materials

Worsted-weight yarn in blue and green (approx 175 total yds)

Size J/10 (6 mm) crochet hook

Small piece of black craft felt

Sewing thread and sharp needle

Black embroidery floss and embroidery needle

Tapestry needle

1"-diameter button

Tiny bit of fiberfill or stuffing of your choice

Eye Roundies (Make 2.)

R1: Using blue yarn, ch 2, sc 5 in second ch from hook.

R2: Sc 2 in every sc around. (10 sts)

R3: *Sc 1, 2 sc in next sc*, rep 5 times. (15 sts)

R4: *Sc 2, 2 sc in next sc*, rep 5 times. (20 sts)

R5: *Sc 3, 2 sc in next sc*, rep 5 times. (25 sts)

R6: Sc 25.

Sl st 1 and fasten off, leaving long tail for sewing. Using the pattern on page 46, cut eye pieces from black felt and sew to middle of roundie; set aside.

Bag/Body

Start crocheting at the nose.

R1: Using green yarn, ch 2, sc 5 in second ch from hook.

R2: Sc 2 in every sc around. (10 sts)

R3: *Sc 1, 2 sc in next sc*, rep 5 times. (15 sts)

R4: *Sc 2, 2 sc in next sc*, rep 5 times. (20 sts)

R5: *Sc 3, 2 sc in next sc*, rep 5 times. (25 sts)

R6: Sc 25.

R7: *Sc 4, 2 sc in next sc*, rep 5 times. (30 sts)

R8: Sc 30.

R9: *Sc 5, 2 sc in next sc*, rep 5 times. (35 sts)

R10: Sc 35.

R11: *Sc 6, 2 sc in next sc*, rep 5 times. (40 sts)

R12: Sc 40.

R13: *Sc 7, 2 sc in next sc*, rep 5 times. (45 sts)

R14: Sc 45.

R15: *Sc 8, 2 sc in next sc*, rep 5 times. (50 sts)

R16: Sc 50.

R17: *Sc 9, 2 sc in next sc*, rep 5 times. (55 sts)

R18: Sc 55.

R19: *Sc 10, 2 sc in next sc*, rep 5 times. (60 sts)

Work on face. Sew eye roundies in place, stuffing them a little. Embroider smile.

Change to blue yarn.

R20: *Sc 11, 2 sc in next sc*, rep 5 times. (65 sts)

R21: Sc 65.

Beg with green yarn, alternate 1 rnd of green and 2 rnds of blue, ending last rnd with blue.

R22: Sc 32, ch 8, sc 33 (button loop made).

Now we'll make the opening. Rather than a zipper, this purse has a loop-and-button closure.

R23: Sc 22, ch 21, sk 21, sc 22.

R24: Sc 22, sc 21 in 21-ch space, sc 22. (65 sts)

Cont with body.

R25–31: Sc 65.

R32: *Sc 11, dec 1*, rep 5 times. (60 sts)

R33: *Sc 10, dec 1*, rep 5 times. (55 sts)

R34: *Sc 9, dec 1*, rep 5 times. (50 sts)

R35: *Sc 8, dec 1*, rep 5 times. (45 sts)

R36 and 37: Sc 45.

R38: *Sc 7, dec 1*, rep 5 times. (40 sts)

R39: Sc 40.

R40: *Sc 6, dec 1*, rep 5 times. (35 sts)

R41: Sc 35.

R42: *Sc 5, dec 1*, rep 5 times. (30 sts)

R43: *Sc 4, dec 1*, rep 5 times. (25 sts)

R44: *Sc 3, dec 1*, rep 5 times. (20 sts)

R45: *Sc 2, dec 1*, rep 5 times. (15 sts)

R46: *Sc 1, dec 1*, rep 5 times. (10 sts)

R47: Dec 5 times. (5 sts)

Fasten off, leaving long tail to close up 5-st hole.

Fins (Make 2.)

R1: Using green yarn, ch 2, sc 6 in second ch from hook.

R2: Sc 2 in every sc around. (12 sts)

R3: *Sc 1, 2 sc in next sc*, rep 6 times. (18 sts)

R4–8: Sc 18.

R9: *Sc 1, dec 1*, rep 6 times. (12 sts)

R10: Sc 12.

R11: Dec 6 times. (6 sts)

Fasten off, leaving long tail for sewing. Sew open end tog and sew to sides on R24.

Tail (Make 2.)

R1: Using green yarn, ch 2, sc 5 in second ch from hook.

R2: Sc 2 in every sc around. (10 sts)

R3: Sc 10.

R4: *Sc 1, 2 sc in next sc*, rep 5 times. (15 sts)

R5: Sc 15.

R6: *Sc 2, 2 sc in next sc*, rep 5 times. (20 sts)

R7–9: Sc 20.

R10: *Sc 2, dec 1*, rep 5 times. (15 sts)

R11: Sc 15.

R12: *Sc 1, dec 1*, rep 5 times. (10 sts)

R13: Sc 10.

R14: Dec 5 times. (5 sts)

Fasten off, leaving long tail for sewing. Sew open end tog. Sew 2 tails tog on last 2 rnds and sew joined tail to end of body.

Handle

Using blue yarn and leaving a long tail for sewing later, loosely ch 91, turn.

Row 1: Sc 90 starting in second ch from hook, turn.

Row 2: Ch 1, sc 90.

Fasten off, leaving long tail for sewing. Sew ends to top of body, one end at R20 and the other end at R39.

Sew button on R28 across from button loop.

Fish eye

Bear Bag in Blue

Finished Size

Approx 8" high x 9½" wide x 1½" deep

I made this one thinking about what I liked when I was a little girl. I used to have a small messenger bag made out of jean material. I loved it and carried it everywhere. So this one is updated with a teddy face, and Oli loves it!

Materials

Worsted-weight yarn in blue and tan (approx 500 total yds)

Size J/10 (6 mm) crochet hook

Small pieces of tan and black craft felt

Sewing thread and sharp needle

Black embroidery floss and embroidery needle

Tapestry needle

Fiberfill or stuffing of your choice 2 wooden 1"-diameter buttons (optional, for decoration)

Bag

All pieces for the bag are worked back and forth.

Use blue yarn for all pieces.

BACK AND FRONT POCKETS (MAKE 2.)

Loosely ch 26.

Row 1: Sc 25 starting in second ch from hook, turn.

Rows 2–25: Ch 1, sc 25, turn.

Fasten off, and set aside.

FRONT

Loosely ch 35.

Row 1: Sc 34 starting in second ch from hook, turn.

Rows 2–35: Ch 1, sc 34, turn.

Fasten off, leaving long tail for sewing. Starting about 5 rows from top, sew sides and bottom of first pocket to WS of front.

BACK AND FRONT OVERLAP

Work as for front through R27.

We will now leave the opening for the back pocket.

Row 28: Ch 1, sc 6, ch 22, sk 22 sts, sc 6, turn.

Row 29: Ch 1, sc 6, sc 22 in 22-ch space, sc 6, turn. (34 sts)

Cont with back.

Rows 30–36: Ch 1, sc 34, turn.

Sew second pocket in place. Align pocket 1 row above opening (row 27) and sew around all 4 sides of rectangle.

Rows 37–74: Ch 1, sc 34, turn.

Row 75: Sc 1 in second sc, sc 30, sk 1 sc, sc 1. (32 sts)

Row 76: Sc 1 in second sc, sc 28, sk 1 sc, sc 1. (30 sts)

Fasten off, and set aside.

BOTTOM

Loosely ch 35.

Row 1: Sc 34 starting in second ch from hook, turn.

Rows 2–7: Ch 1, sc 34, turn.

Fasten off, and set aside.

SIDES (MAKE 2.)

Loosely ch 27.

Row 1: Sc 26 starting in second ch from hook, turn.

Rows 2–7: Ch 1, sc 26, turn.

Fasten off, and set aside.

PUTTING THE PIECES TOGETHER

Using blue yarn and tapestry needle, place pieces WS tog and use whipstitch (see page 76) to join bottom and sides to front of bag. Then join small ends of bottom to sides. Sew the back of bag to the unit.

HANDLE

Using blue yarn, loosely ch 103.

Row 1: Sc 102 starting in second ch from hook, turn.

Rows 2–7: Ch 1, sc 102, turn.

Fasten off, leaving long tail for sewing. Sew one end to top of each side. If desired, add decorative wooden buttons where handle was joined.

Bear Face

R1: Using tan yarn, ch 2, sc 5 in second ch from hook.

R2: Sc 2 in every sc around. (10 sts)

R3: *Sc 1, 2 sc in next sc*, rep 5 times. (15 sts)

R4: *Sc 2, 2 sc in next sc*, rep 5 times. (20 sts)

R5: *Sc 3, 2 sc in next sc*, rep 5 times. (25 sts)

R6: *Sc 4, 2 sc in next sc*, rep 5 times. (30 sts)

R7: *Sc 5, 2 sc in next sc*, rep 5 times. (35 sts)

R8: *Sc 6, 2 sc in next sc*, rep 5 times. (40 sts)

R9: *Sc 7, 2 sc in next sc*, rep 5 times. (45 sts)

R10: *Sc 8, 2 sc in next sc*, rep 5 times. (50 sts)

R11: *Sc 9, 2 sc in next sc*, rep 5 times. (55 sts)

R12 and 13: Sc 55.

Sl st 1 and fasten off, leaving long tail for sewing.

Using pattern on facing page, cut muzzle from tan felt.

Embroider nose and smile. Cut eye pieces from black felt and sew in place.

Centering face on front of bag, stitch approx ¾ of the way around, stuff a little, and finish sewing.

Ears (Make 2.)

R1: Using tan yarn, ch 2, sc 5 in second ch from hook.

R2: Sc 2 in every sc around. (10 sts)

R3 and 4: Sc 10.

Fasten off, leaving long tail for sewing. Sew ears to face.

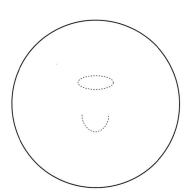

Bear muzzle

Bear eye

Cupcake and Ladybug Snack Bags

Finished Size

Cupcake: Approx 5¾" high
Ladybug: Approx 5" high

These are actually big enough to carry lunch, making them a great alternative to paper bags. (Plus, they're a lot cuter!)

Materials

Cupcake: Worsted-weight yarn in pink, tan, and a bit of red (approx 120 total yds)

Ladybug: Worsted-weight yarn in red, black, and white (approx 120 total yds)

Size J/10 (6 mm) crochet hook

Small piece of black craft felt

Sewing thread and sharp needle

Black and red embroidery floss and embroidery needle

Tapestry needle

Tiny bit of fiberfill or stuffing of your choice

Cupcake

Start crocheting at the bottom of the bag.

R1: Using tan yarn, ch 2, sc 6 in second ch from hook.

R2: Sc 2 in every sc around. (12 sts)

R3: *Sc 1, 2 sc in next sc*, rep 6 times. (18 sts)

R4: *Sc 2, 2 sc in next sc*, rep 6 times. (24 sts)

R5: *Sc 3, 2 sc in next sc*, rep 6 times. (30 sts)

R6: *Sc 4, 2 sc in next sc*, rep 6 times. (36 sts)

R7: *Sc 5, 2 sc in next sc*, rep 6 times. (42 sts)

R8: *Sc 6, 2 sc in next sc*, rep 6 times. (48 sts)

R9: *Sc 7, 2 sc in next sc*, rep 6 times. (54 sts)

R10: *Sc 8, 2 sc in next sc*, rep 6 times. (60 sts)

R11: Through back loops only: *Sc 8, dec 1*, rep 6 times. (54 sts)

R12: *Sc 8, 2 sc in next sc*, rep 6 times. (60 sts)

R13–20: Sc 60.

Work on face. Using pattern on facing page, cut eye pieces from black felt and sew in place. Embroider smile.

Change to pink yarn.

R21: Sc 60 through front loops only.

R22: Hdc 60 through back loops only.

R23–26: Hdc 60.

R27: *Hdc 8, hdc dec 1*, rep 6 times. (54 sts)

R28: *Hdc 7, hdc dec 1*, rep 6 times. (48 sts)

R29: *Hdc 6, hdc dec 1*, rep 6 times. (42 sts)

R30: *Hdc 5, hdc dec 1*, rep 6 times. (36 sts)

R31: *Hdc 4, hdc dec 1*, rep 6 times. (30 sts)

R32 and 33: Sc 30.

R34: Hdc 1, *ch 1, sk 1 hdc, hdc 1*, rep all the way around, sl st 1.

Fasten off.

WAVY EDGE

Join pink yarn to one of the front loops you left in R22.

Ch 4, 2 hdc in next hdc, sk 1 hdc, sl st 1, *3 hdc in next hdc, sk 1 hdc, sl st 1*, rep all the way around. Sl st 1 and fasten off.

CORD

Using pink yarn, loosely ch 71.

Sl st 70 starting in second ch from hook.

Fasten off. Weave cord in and out of ch-1 spaces at top of bag. Pull ends to close bag.

CHERRIES (MAKE 2.)

R1: Using red yarn, ch 2, 6 sc in second ch from hook.

R2: Sc 2 in each st around. (12 sts)

R3–6: Sc 12.

Stuff a little.

R7: Dec 6 times. (6 sts)

Fasten off, leaving long tail for sewing. Stuff a little more and sew one to each end of cord.

Ladybug

Begin with the eye roundies.

EYE ROUNDIES (MAKE 2.)

R1: Using white yarn, ch 2, sc 5 in second ch from hook.

R2: Sc 2 in every sc around. (10 sts)

R3 and 4: Sc 10.

Sl st 1 and fasten off, leaving long tail for sewing.

Using pattern on facing page, cut eye pieces from black felt, sew one to center of each roundie, and set aside.

BAG/BODY

R1: Using black yarn, ch 2, sc 6 in second ch from hook.

R2: Sc 2 in every sc around. (12 sts)

R3: *Sc 1, 2 sc in next sc*, rep 6 times. (18 sts)

R4: *Sc 2, 2 sc in next sc*, rep 6 times. (24 sts)

R5: *Sc 3, 2 sc in next sc*, rep 6 times. (30 sts)

R6: *Sc 4, 2 sc in next sc*, rep 6 times. (36 sts)

R7: *Sc 5, 2 sc in next sc*, rep 6 times. (42 sts)

R8: *Sc 6, 2 sc in next sc*, rep 6 times. (48 sts)

R9: *Sc 7, 2 sc in next sc*, rep 6 times. (54 sts)

R10: *Sc 8, 2 sc in next sc*, rep 6 times. (60 sts)

R11–18: Sc 60.

Change to red.

R19 and 20: Hdc 60.

Work on face. Sew eyes in place and embroider smile.

R21 and 22: Hdc 60.

R23: *Hdc 8, hdc dec 1*, rep 6 times. (54 sts)

R24: *Hdc 7, hdc dec 1*, rep 6 times. (48 sts)

R25: *Hdc 6, hdc dec 1*, rep 6 times. (42 sts)

R26: *Hdc 5, hdc dec 1*, rep 6 times. (36 sts)

R27: *Hdc 4, hdc dec 1*, rep 6 times. (30 sts)

R28 and 29: Hdc 30.

R30: Hdc 1, *ch 1, sk 1 hdc, hdc 1*, rep all the way around, sl st 1.

Fasten off and weave in loose ends.

Using black yarn and a crochet hook, crochet a line of chain stitches (see below) in the middle of the red section, between the eyes. With the yarn on the inside of the bag, insert the hook in a stitch on the last rnd of the black section, yarn over hook, and pull through to front. *Insert the hook into next stitch 1 rnd above, yarn over hook, and pull through to front, then pull through the loop on the hook. Rep from * up to the second rnd from the top. Fasten off. Make another line on the back of the bag the same way.

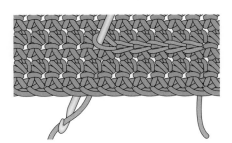

SPOTS (MAKE 10.)

R1: Using black yarn, ch 2, sc 5 in second ch from hook.

R2: Sc 2 in every sc around. (10 sts)

Sl st 1 and fasten off, leaving long tail for sewing. Sew them to red section.

CORD

Using red yarn, loosely ch 71. Sl st 70 starting in second ch from hook.

Fasten off. Weave cord in and out of ch-1 spaces at top of bag. Pull ends to close bag.

Cupcake eye

Ladybug eye

Colorful Little Duffel

Finished Size

Approx 5" high x 9" wide

This one is for Oli, who is a great student and always reading, and at the same time is very fashionable and so into what "looks good." I'm amazed at how fast she's growing. Here I am, living with a tiny teenager who likes to paint her nails! I still see her as a little girl—and she is, after all—so I had to add the little teddy face.

Materials

Worsted-weight yarn in blue, yellow, orange, red, pink, green, gray, and brown (approx 250 total yds)

Size J/10 (6 mm) crochet hook

Small piece of tan craft felt

Black embroidery floss and embroidery needle

6 mm plastic eyes with safety backings

Tapestry needle

Tiny bit of fiberfill or stuffing of your choice

10"-long zipper

Bag

Beg with blue yarn, alternate 3 rows each of blue, yellow, orange, red, pink, green, and gray. The bag is worked back and forth

Loosely ch 33.

Row 1: Sc 32 starting in second ch from hook, turn.

Rows 2–66: Ch 1, sc 32, turn.

Fasten off.

Ends (Make 2.)

R1: Using blue yarn and working in the rnd, ch 2, sc 5 in second ch from hook.

R2: Sc 2 in every sc around. (10 sts)

R3: *Sc 1, 2 sc in next sc*, rep 5 times. (15 sts)

R4: *Sc 2, 2 sc in next sc*, rep 5 times. (20 sts)

R5: *Sc 3, 2 sc in next sc*, rep 5 times. (25 sts)

R6: *Sc 4, 2 sc in next sc*, rep 5 times. (30 sts)

R7: *Sc 5, 2 sc in next sc*, rep 5 times. (35 sts)

R8: *Sc 6, 2 sc in next sc*, rep 5 times. (40 sts)

R9: *Sc 7, 2 sc in next sc*, rep 5 times. (45 sts)

R10: *Sc 8, 2 sc in next sc*, rep 5 times. (50 sts)

R11: Sc 50.

Fasten off, leaving long tail for sewing.

Putting the Pieces Together

Using blue yarn and tapestry needle, place pieces RS tog, and use whipstitch (see page 76) to join ends to bag, leaving top of bag open for the zipper. Sew zipper in place (see page 76).

Handle

Use blue yarn. Working back and forth and leaving a long tail for sewing later, loosely chain 81.

Row 1: Sc 80 starting in second ch from hook, turn.

Rows 2–5: Sc 1, sc 80, turn.

Fasten off, leaving long tail for sewing. Sew one end to each end of bag, 3 rnds below zipper opening.

Bear Head

Use brown yarn.

HEAD

Start crocheting at the top of the head, working in the rnd.

R1: Ch 2, sc 5 in second ch from hook.

R2: Sc 2 in every sc around. (10 sts)

R3: *Sc 1, 2 sc in next sc*, rep 5 times. (15 sts)

R4: *Sc 2, 2 sc in next sc*, rep 5 times. (20 sts)

R5–9: Sc 20.

Work on face. Using pattern at right, cut muzzle from tan felt.

Embroider nose and smile. Position and attach plastic eyes with safety backings.

R10: *Sc 2, dec 1*, rep 5 times. (15 sts)

R11: *Sc 1, dec 1*, rep 5 times. (10 sts)

Stuff head.

R12: Dec 5 times. (5 sts)

Fasten off.

EARS (MAKE 2.)

Ch 2, sc 7 in second ch from hook.

Fasten off, leaving long tail for sewing. Sew to head.

Insert a piece of yarn through the top of bear's head (with the help of a hook), attach to zipper pull, and tie a knot.

Bear muzzle

Cute Apple Cozies

Finished Size

Approx 3" tall

Apples can get cold, you know? Well, not really, but these little "sweaters" do protect them from all the bumps they suffer inside backpacks when they're traveling to school! Wouldn't one of these make a cute present for a teacher too?

Materials

Worsted-weight yarn in gray, pink, orange, yellow, and blue (approx 50 yds per cozy)

Size G/6 (4 mm) crochet hook

Small pieces of white, tan, and black craft felt

Black, brown, and pink embroidery floss and embroidery needle

Tapestry needle

½"-diameter button

Cozy

Start crocheting at the bottom of the cozy.

R1: Using gray, pink, orange, yellow, or blue yarn, ch 2, sc 6 in second ch from hook.

R2: 2 sc in every sc around. (12 sts)

R3: *Sc 1, 2 sc in next sc*, rep 6 times. (18 sts)

R4: *Sc 2, 2 sc in next sc*, rep 6 times. (24 sts)

R5: *Sc 3, 2 sc in next sc*, rep 6 times. (30 sts)

R6: *Sc 4, 2 sc in next sc*, rep 6 times. (36 sts)

R7–11: Sc 36.

R12: Sc 36, turn.

From now on, work back and forth through *front loops only.*

Row 13: Ch 1, sc 36, turn.

Row 14: Ch 1, *sc 4, dec 1*, rep 6 times, turn. (30 sts)

Rows 15–17: Ch 1, sc 30, turn.

Row 18: Ch 1, sc 30, ch 20, and now we'll sc all around the opening: sl st in the same st you started the 20 ch, sc 8 down the right side of the opening, sc 2 in the corner of the opening, sc 8 up the left side of the opening, sl st 1 and fasten off.

Sew button to opposite side of loop.

Face

Use patterns on page 62.

For koala, cut nose and eye pieces from black felt and sew in place. Embroider smile.

For bunny and cat, cut muzzle pieces from white or tan felt, embroider nose and smile, and sew in place. Cut eye pieces from black felt and sew in place. Embroider whiskers on cat's face.

For chick, cut beak piece from tan felt. Fold in half and stitch in place on the crease. Cut eye pieces from black felt and sew in place.

For owl, cut beak from tan felt and sew in place. Cut eye pieces from black and white felt, sew black pieces slightly off center on white pieces, and sew in place.

KOALA EARS (MAKE 2.)

R1: Using gray yarn, ch 2, sc 5 in second ch from hook.

R2: 2 sc in every sc around. (10 sts)

R3: *Sc 1, 2 sc in next sc*, rep 5 times. (15 sts)

R4–6: Sc 15.

Fasten off, leaving long tail for sewing. Sew open end tog and sew one to each side.

BUNNY EARS (MAKE 2.)

R1: Using pink yarn, ch 2, sc 5 in second ch from hook.

R2: 2 sc in every sc around. (10 sts)

R3–10: Sc 10.

Fasten off, leaving long tail for sewing. Sew open end tog and sew one to each side.

CAT EARS (MAKE 2.)

R1: Using orange yarn, ch 2, sc 5 in second ch from hook.

R2: Sc 5.

R3: 2 sc in every sc around. (10 sts)

R4: Sc 10.

Fasten off, leaving long tail for sewing. Sew open end tog and sew one to top on each side.

CHICK AND OWL WINGS (MAKE 2.)

R1: Using yellow or blue yarn, ch 2, sc 5 in second ch from hook.

R2: Sc 5.

R3: 2 sc in every sc around. (10 sts)

R4–7: Sc 10.

Fasten off, leaving long tail for sewing. Sew open end tog and sew one to each side.

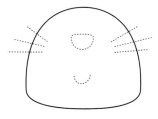

Owl outer eye

Eyes

Chick beak

Owl beak

Koala nose

Cat nose

Bunny nose

Carrot and Tomato Coin Purses

Finished Size

Carrot: Approx 4" high
Tomato: Approx 3" high

I have the cutest wallet, but even though it has a place for coins, they always end up in the bottom of my purse. These darling little coin purses will definitely solve the problem, and they're an ideal place to keep the tiny little toys (or rocks, or pieces of paper, or tiny leaves!) that Martina still carries around wherever we go.

Materials

Worsted-weight yarn in orange, red, and a bit of green (approx 50 total yds per purse)

Size J/10 (6 mm) crochet hook

Small piece of black craft felt

Sewing thread and sharp needle

Black embroidery floss and embroidery needle

Tapestry needle

6"-long zipper

Carrot

Start crocheting at the bottom of the carrot.

R1: Using orange yarn, ch 2, sc 5 in second ch from hook.

R2: 2 sc in every sc around. (10 sts)

R3: *Sc 1, 2 sc in next sc*, rep 5 times. (15 sts)

R4 and 5: Sc 15.

R6: *Sc 2, 2 sc in next sc*, rep 5 times. (20 sts)

R7–9: Sc 20.

R10: *Sc 3, 2 sc in next sc*, rep 5 times. (25 sts)

R11: Sc 25.

R12: *Sc 4, 2 sc in next sc*, rep 5 times. (30 sts)

R13–15: Sc 30.

R16: *Sc 5, 2 sc in next sc*, rep 5 times. (35 sts)

R17: Sc 35.

We will now work on the opening for the zipper.

R18: Ch 15, sk 15 sts, sc 20.

R19: Sc 15 in 15-ch space, sc 20. (35 sts)

Work on face. Using pattern on page 65, cut eye pieces from black felt and sew in place. Embroider smile.

R20: *Sc 5, dec 1*, rep 5 times. (30 sts)

R21: *Sc 4, dec 1*, rep 5 times. (25 sts)

Sew zipper in place (see page 76).

R22: *Sc 3, dec 1*, rep 5 times. (20 sts)

R23: *Sc 2, dec 1*, rep 5 times. (15 sts)

R24: *Sc 1, dec 1*, rep 5 times. (10 sts)

R25: Dec 5 times. (5 sts)

Fasten off, leaving long tail to close up 5-st hole.

Carrot Leaves

Using green yarn, *ch 15, fold to form a loop, join to the base with a sl st*, rep 5 times.

Sew all loops together at the base, and sew to top of carrot.

Tomato

Start crocheting at the top of the tomato.

R1: Using red yarn, ch 2, sc 5 in second ch from hook.

R2: 2 sc in every sc around. (10 sts)

R3: *Sc 1, 2 sc in next sc*, rep 5 times. (15 sts)

R4: *Sc 2, 2 sc in next sc*, rep 5 times. (20 sts)

R5: *Sc 3, 2 sc in next sc*, rep 5 times. (25 sts)

R6: *Sc 4, 2 sc in next sc*, rep 5 times. (30 sts)

R7: *Sc 5, 2 sc in next sc*, rep 5 times. (35 sts)

R8: Sc 35.

We will now work on the opening for the zipper.

R9: Ch 15, sk 15 sts, sc 20.

R10: Sc 15 in 15-ch space, sc 20. (35 sts)

R11–16: Sc 35.

Sew zipper in place (see page 76).

Work on face. Using pattern at bottom right, cut eye pieces from black felt and sew in place. Embroider smile.

R17: *Sc 5, dec 1*, rep 5 times. (30 sts)

R18: *Sc 4, dec 1*, rep 5 times. (25 sts)

R19: *Sc 3, dec 1*, rep 5 times. (20 sts)

R20: *Sc 2, dec 1*, rep 5 times. (15 sts)

R21: *Sc 1, dec 1*, rep 5 times. (10 sts)

R22: Dec 5 times. (5 sts)

Fasten off, leaving long tail to close up 5-st hole.

Tomato Leaves

Use green yarn for leaves and stem.

For leaves, *ch 6, sc 5 starting at second ch from hook*, rep 6 times; ch 4, sl st 3 for stem.

Fasten off, leaving long tail for sewing. Sew to top of tomato.

Carrot and Tomato eye

Turtle Lunch Tote

Finished Size

Approx 10" high, including legs

Your little one will be so happy to let this friendly turtle carry lunch to school every day. Now we just need a way to find out if lunch really gets eaten before dessert, and we'll be happy too!

Materials

Worsted-weight yarn in light green, dark blue, and 2 contrasting colors (approx 250 total yds)

Size J/10 (6 mm) crochet hook

12 mm plastic eyes with safety backings,

Sewing thread and sharp needle

Black embroidery floss and embroidery needle

Tapestry needle

Body

R1: Using light-green yarn, ch 2, sc 5 in second ch from hook.

R2: 2 sc in every sc around. (10 sts)

R3: *Sc 1, 2 sc in next sc*, rep 5 times. (15 sts)

R4: *Sc 2, 2 sc in next sc*, rep 5 times. (20 sts)

R5: *Sc 3, 2 sc in next sc*, rep 5 times. (25 sts)

R6: *Sc 4, 2 sc in next sc*, rep 5 times. (30 sts)

R7: *Sc 5, 2 sc in next sc*, rep 5 times. (35 sts)

R8: *Sc 6, 2 sc in next sc*, rep 5 times. (40 sts)

R9: *Sc 7, 2 sc in next sc*, rep 5 times. (45 sts)

R10: *Sc 8, 2 sc in next sc*, rep 5 times. (50 sts)

R11: *Sc 9, 2 sc in next sc*, rep 5 times. (55 sts)

R12: *Sc 10, 2 sc in next sc*, rep 5 times. (60 sts)

R13: *Sc 11, 2 sc in next sc*, rep 5 times. (65 sts)

R14: *Sc 12, 2 sc in next sc*, rep 5 times. (70 sts)

R15: Sc 70 through back loops only.

R16–21: Sc 70.

Change to dark blue.

R22–31: Hdc 70.

R32: *Hdc 12, hdc dec 1*, rep 5 times. (65 sts)

R33: Hdc 65.

R34: *Hdc 11, hdc dec 1*, rep 5 times. (60 sts)

R35: Hdc 60.

R36: *Hdc 10, hdc dec 1*, rep 5 times. (55 sts)

R37: *Hdc 9, hdc dec 1*, rep 5 times. (50 sts)

R38: *Hdc 8, hdc dec 1*, rep 5 times. (45 sts)

R39: *Hdc 7, hdc dec 1*, rep 5 times. (40 sts)

R40: *Dc 6, dc dec 1*, rep 5 times. (35 sts)

Fasten off.

Stripes

Refer to page 39 of the Whale Bag instructions for illustration of weaving yarn, except work in hdc section on turtle using different colors. With tapestry needle and starting at bottom of blue section with one of your contrasting-color yarns (dark green in the project shown), weave yarn over and under hdc on every rnd, alternating the placement of over and under from rnd to rnd. Work 1 rnd of this color and 2 rnds of your second contrasting color (orange in project shown) for a total of 12 stripes.

Head

R1: Using light-green yarn, ch 2, sc 5 in second ch from hook.

R2: 2 sc in every sc around. (10 sts)

R3: *Sc 1, 2 sc in next sc*, rep 5 times. (15 sts)

R4: *Sc 2, 2 sc in next sc*, rep 5 times. (20 sts)

R5: *Sc 3, 2 sc in next sc*, rep 5 times. (25 sts)

R6–11: Sc 25.

R12: *Sc 3, dec 1*, rep 5 times. (20 sts)

R13–15: Sc 20.

Fasten off, leaving long tail for sewing.

Face

Position and attach plastic eyes with safety backings, embroider smile, stuff head, and sew to front of body. Attach 11th rnd of head to third rnd of hdc; this will keep the head up.

Legs (Make 4.)

R1: Using light-green yarn, ch 2, sc 5 in second ch from hook.

R2: 2 sc in every sc around. (10 sts)

R3: *Sc 1, 2 sc in next sc*, rep 5 times. (15 sts)

R4–12: Sc 15.

Fasten off, leaving long tail for sewing. Stuff a little, sew open end together, and sew to R15 on bottom.

Cord

Using one of your contrasting-color yarns (orange in the project shown), loosely ch 81, sl st 80 starting in second ch from hook.

Fasten off.

Weave cord over 2 sts and under 2 sts all around top, leave 5 dc without cord at front of bag. Tie a knot in each end of cord. Pull ends to close bag.

General Guidelines

Simple crochet skills are all you need to make these delightful amigurumi accessories.

Yarn

The accessories in this book are crocheted using worsted-weight yarn and a size J/10 (6 mm) crochet hook, plus occasionally a size G/6 (4 mm) hook.

I used cotton yarn for these projects because bags and everyday accessories that kids might take to school tend to get very dirty, and cotton seems to hold up better than wool when put in the washing machine. Also, I don't know about your kids, but mine are always hot (oh, to be young again!). I couldn't imagine either of them carrying a warm backpack in the summer, so cotton seemed like a better option.

A list of the yarn brands I used for the samples in this book can be found on page 78, but it doesn't really matter which brand you use. Choose colors similar to mine, or be creative and come up with your own color combinations!

Gauge, Tension, and Hook Sizes

The measurements given for each project are approximate and based on the way I crochet. I crochet pretty tightly, and with a J hook and worsted-weight yarn, my gauge is as follows:

35 sc and 7 rounds =
3" diameter circle
50 sc and 10 rounds =
4"-diameter circle

The finished size, however, isn't really that important, so don't worry if your gauge is different from mine. Depending on your tension and the yarn you use, your bag or purse might end up being a little bit smaller or larger than the ones I made. Changing to a bigger or smaller hook will give you a bigger or smaller accessory, respectively.

Stitches

Simple stitches are used for these amigurumi projects, making them perfect for beginners.

Chain (ch). Make a slipknot and place it on the hook. Yarn over the hook, draw the yarn through the slipknot, and let the slipknot slide off the hook. *Yarn over the hook, draw the yarn through the new loop, and let the loop slide off the hook. Repeat from * for the desired number of chain sts.

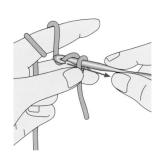

Slip stitch (sl st). A slip stitch is used to move across one or more stitches. Insert the hook into the stitch, yarn over the hook, and pull through both loops on the hook at once.

Single crochet (sc). *Insert the hook into the chain or stitch indicated, yarn over the hook, and pull through the chain or stitch (two loops on the hook).

Yarn over the hook and pull through the two loops on the hook. Repeat from * for the required number of stitches.

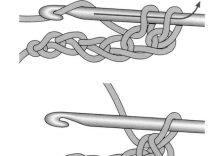

Single crochet increase. Work two single crochet stitches into the same stitch.

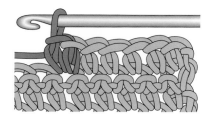

Single crochet decrease (dec 1). (Insert the hook into the next stitch, yarn over, pull up a loop) twice; yarn over and pull through all three loops on the hook.

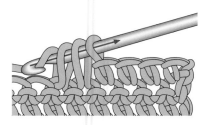

Half double crochet (hdc). *Yarn over the hook and insert the hook into the chain or stitch indicated. Yarn over the hook and pull through the stitch (three loops on the hook).

Yarn over the hook and pull through all three loops on the hook. Repeat from * for the required number of stitches.

Half double crochet increase. Work two half double crochet stitches into the same stitch.

Half double crochet decrease (hdc dec 1). *Yarn over the hook and insert the hook into the next stitch, yarn over the hook and pull through the stitch (three loops on the hook). Yarn over the hook and insert the hook into the next stitch, yarn over the hook and pull through the stitch. Yarn over the hook and pull through all five loops on the hook.

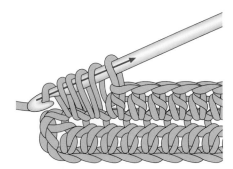

Double crochet (dc). *Yarn over the hook and insert the hook into the chain or stitch indicated. Yarn over the hook and pull through the stitch (three loops on the hook); yarn over the hook and pull through two loops

on the hook (two loops on the hook).

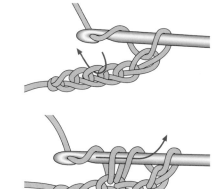

Yarn over the hook and pull through the remaining two loops on the hook (one loop on the hook). Repeat from * for the required number of stitches.

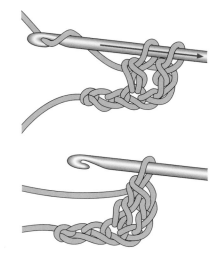

Double crochet decrease (dc dec 1). Yarn over hook and insert the hook into the next stitch, yarn over hook and pull through the stitch, yarn over the hook and pull through two loops on the hook (two loops on the hook).

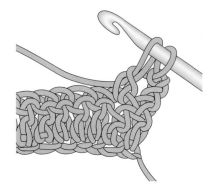

Yarn over the hook, insert the hook into the next stitch, yarn over the hook and pull through the stitch, yarn over the hook and pull through two loops on the hook (three loops on the hook).

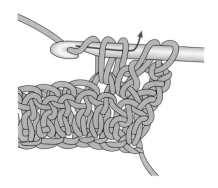

Yarn over the hook and pull through all three loops on the hook.

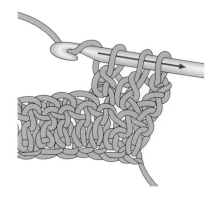

Working in Chain Loops

When crocheting the first row into the beginning chain, the first row of stitches is generally worked into one or both loops on the right side of the chain.

Crocheting into top loop

Crocheting into both loops

For some projects, the first row of stitches is worked in the "bump" on the wrong side of the chain.

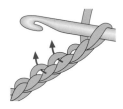

Working in Stitch Loops

The majority of the stitches are worked in both loops of the stitches from the previous row. There are a few projects where you will work into the back loop or the front loop of the stitch.

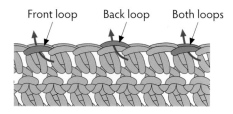

Front loop   Back loop   Both loops

Crocheting in the Round

When crocheting in the round, I crochet around and around, forming a continuous spiral without joining rounds. To keep track of where the rounds begin and end, you can mark the end or beginning of a round with a safety pin, stitch marker, or little piece of yarn pulled through one of the stitches. At the end of the last round, slip stitch in the first single crochet of the previous round and fasten off the yarn.

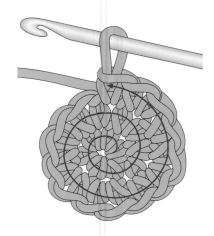

How to Change Yarn Colors

Some projects require alternating two colors in the body. To do this, work the last stitch of a round until one step remains in the stitch; then work the last step with the new color and continue the round in the new color. Continue to the end of the round and change color in the same manner.

Adding Faces

The templates for the muzzles and any other pieces to be cut from felt are included with each project. Cut the felt pieces with sharp scissors to get nice, smooth edges. Using embroidery floss and a needle, I use simple stitches to "draw" the faces on the felt before attaching the felt pieces to the accessories. Sew pieces of felt on with a sharp needle and matching sewing thread. Use a very small running stitch close to the edge of the piece.

MOUTHS

For a simple mouth, bring the needle out at point A and insert the needle at point B, leaving a loose strand of floss to form the mouth. Once you're happy with the shape of the mouth, bring the needle out again at point C, cross over the loose strand of floss, and insert the needle at point D to make a tiny stitch. Secure the ends on the wrong side.

NOSES AND EYES

To satin stitch features, bring the needle out through point A, insert at point B, and repeat, following the shape you want for the nose or eyes and making sure to work the stitches really close together. Secure the ends on the wrong side.

Another option for embroidering a nose is to work from a center point upward (like for the Owl Bag at bottom right). Bring the needle up from underneath at point A; insert the needle at point B. Bring the needle up at point C, very close to point A. Insert the needle back into point B. Continue working stitches close to each other to create a triangle, making sure to always insert the needle back into point B. When you're satisfied with the triangle, make two long stitches across the top of the nose to help define it.

Stuffing

I always use polyester fiberfill stuffing because it's nonallergenic, won't bunch up, and it's washable, which is always good when you're making things that may get washed often! If you do wash these items, make sure you follow the care instructions on the yarn label.

Adding the Extremities

I always use a tapestry needle and the same color of yarn as the pieces (or at least one of the pieces) that I want to sew together. When joining pieces, make sure they are securely attached so that little fingers can't pull them off.

On some bags, the opening of the animal extremities will remain open for sewing onto the body; the instructions will tell you when to leave them open. Position the limb on the bag/body and sew all around it, going through the front stitches of both the limb and the body.

On other bags, the opening of the extremities will be sewn closed before being attached to the body. To do this, pinch the opening closed, line up the stitches of one side with the other side, and sew through the front loop of one side and the back loop of the other side. Position the piece where you want it on the bag/body and sew.

Whipstitch

This easy stitch is used in some of the projects to sew pieces together.

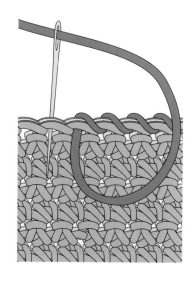

Adding Zippers

Sewing zippers is a lot easier than it seems! With the right side of the project facing you, align the zipper (from the inside of the bag) with its opening. Make sure the zipper pull is touching one of the ends so you won't have a hole in the corner. Close the zipper and baste it in place with a sewing needle and contrasting-color sewing thread (so it's easier to see). Once you're done, sew it in place with a tapestry needle and yarn to match the bag. Sew one side, and then open it and sew the other side. Presto! (See photo on page 19.)

Don't worry if your zipper is longer than the opening. You can either leave the extra part inside the bag or trim it off, making sure you secure the end with a lot of tight stitches.

Weaving in Ends

When you bind off your work, make sure to leave a tail 4" long so that you'll be able to hide it in the back. Using a tapestry needle and working on the wrong side of the project, insert the needle into the bottom row of stitches, sliding it behind the two loops of each stitch until you have a little piece left. The shorter the piece, the better, so that you won't have to cut it with scissors and risk cutting your just-finished work!

Abbreviations and Glossary

*	repeat directions between * and * as many times as indicated
approx	approximately
beg	beginning
ch	chain
cont	continue
dc	double crochet
dc dec 1	double crochet 2 stitches together (see page 73)
dec 1	single crochet 2 stitches together (see page 72)
hdc	half double crochet
hdc dec 1	half double crochet 2 stitches together (see page 73)
R	round(s)
rep	repeat
rnd(s)	round(s)
RS	right side
sc	single crochet
sk	skip
sl st	slip stitch
st(s)	stitch(es)
tog	together
WS	wrong side

Resources

Yarn

Bernat
www.bernat.com
Handicrafter Cotton

Lily Sugar'n Cream
www.sugarncream.com
Sugar'n Cream

Lion Brand Yarn
www.lionbrand.com
Cotton-Ease

Safety Eyes

I only used safety eyes in a couple of projects in this book and used felt instead, but you can always use plastic eyes if you like them better. Your local craft store probably carries safety eyes. If you can't find them locally, visit www.sunshinecrafts.com; search for "eyes." They ship them fast. If you want fun, colorful eyes, check out www.suncatchereyes.net.

Zippers

I had the worst time finding the right zippers on the internet, and ended up buying the nicest, most colorful ones in this Etsy shop: www.kandcsupplies.etsy.com

Acknowledgments

Thank you to everyone at Martingale for being so nice, kind, and talented, and for making my work look beautiful!

It's a real pleasure to work with you.

Thank you from the bottom of my heart.

Hugs!

What's your creative passion?

Find it at **ShopMartingale.com**

books • eBooks • ePatterns • daily blog • free projects
videos • tutorials • inspiration • giveaways

Martingale
Create with Confidence